All About
Virtual
Reality

Written by Jack Challoner

Written by Jack Challoner
Curiscope Ben Kidd and Ed Barton

Senior editor Sam Priddy
Senior art editor Fiona Macdonald
Designer Emma Hobson
Design assistants Rhea Gaughan,
Bettina Myklebust Stovne, Ala Uddin
Jacket co-ordinator Francesca Young
Jacket designer Elle Ward
Managing editors Laura Gilbert, Deborah Lock
Managing art editors Diane Peyton Jones,
Vicky Short
Picture researcher Aditya Katyal
Pre-production producer Nikoleta Parasaki
Viewer developer Toby Marshall
Senior producer Isabell Schart
Production manager Andy Beehag
Art director Martin Wilson
Publisher Sarah Larter
Design director Phil Ormerod
Publishing director Sophie Mitchell

First published in Great Britain in 2017 by
Dorling Kindersley Limited
80 Strand, London, WC2R 0RL

A CIP catalogue record for this book
is available from the British Library.
ISBN: 978-0-2413-0903-2

Printed and bound in China

A WORLD OF IDEAS:
SEE ALL THERE IS TO KNOW

www.dk.com

Contents

How to download the app

In order to experience virtual reality with this book, you will need to ask a parent or guardian to download the **DK Virtual Reality** app from the App Store (iOS) or Google Play. It is free of charge. Links to the app can be found at:
www.dk.com/virtualreality

Minimum OS version: iOS 8.3
and Android 4.4.4

The following phones support the app: iPhone 6; 6 Plus; 6s; 6s Plus; 7; Samsung Galaxy S5; S6; S7; S8; Samsung Galaxy Note 4; 5; Motorola Moto X; Motorola Droid Turbo; LG G3; G4; G5; G6; Google Pixel; HTC One; Nexus 5; Nexus 6; Sony Xperia Z3; Z5.

If your phone is not on this list, the app may still work. Devices must have rear camera and support OpenGL ES 2.0. See device manufacturer for more information.

Safety message

It is important to be sensible when using the virtual reality viewer. Please read the safety tips here before assembling the viewer and using the virtual reality app.

- **Young children should always be supervised by an adult when using virtual reality.**

- **Do not spend more than 15 minutes using virtual reality at any time.**

- **If you are experiencing nausea, discomfort, eye strain, or disorientation, stop using the viewer immediately.**

- **Take frequent breaks when using the virtual reality viewer.**

- **Do not use the virtual reality viewer outside, or in any way that could distract you from real-world situations, such as walking on stairs. Preferably sit down when using the viewer. If you want to stand up, make sure you are supervised by an adult at all times.**

- **If you suffer from seizures, please consult a doctor before using the virtual reality viewer.**

- **Do not point the virtual reality viewer directly at the sun, or leave the viewer in direct sunlight.**

Virtual reality can take you to places you would not normally be able to visit!

Looking into a VR headset is like looking into a different world.

What is virtual reality?

Your brain uses information from your eyes and ears to sense reality – the world around you. In virtual reality (VR), a headset produces sights and sounds from virtual worlds created on computers, fooling you into thinking you are somewhere else.

As you move your head, you look around the virtual world.

The things you see in VR can appear so real you believe you can reach out and touch them.

The things you see in the virtual world are not really there!

Timeline

Virtual reality only became widely available in the 2010s, but its history stretches back more than 50 years.

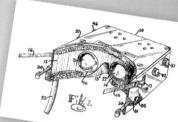

1957 Sensorama, an early VR viewer, displays images and sound.

1980 The US Air Force uses a Super Cockpit VR device in pilot training.

1990s The development of VR slows down because computers are too slow and expensive.

2012 Oculus VR is founded. The Oculus Rift headset will kickstart the VR revolution.

2014 Google invents an affordable VR headset, called Google Cardboard.

2015 A big year for VR, as many new headsets become available.

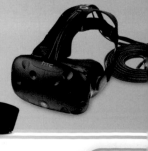

How to make your viewer

To begin assembling your viewer, first lay out all the pieces shown below. It is best to make this viewer on a hard surface, such as a table.

Pieces

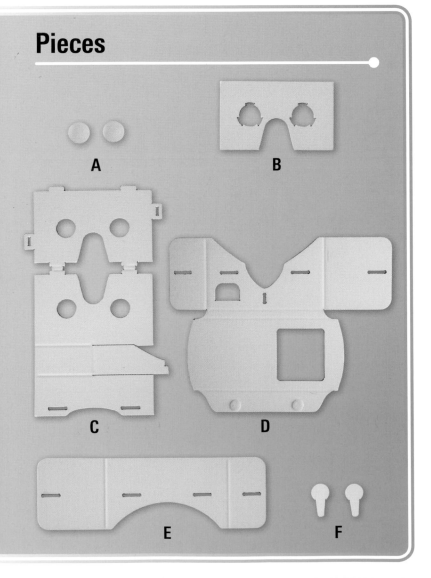

A

B

C

D

E

F

Place the lenses (**A**) into the eyeholes of piece **B**. The lenses have a flat side and a curved side. Make sure both lenses are the same way round.

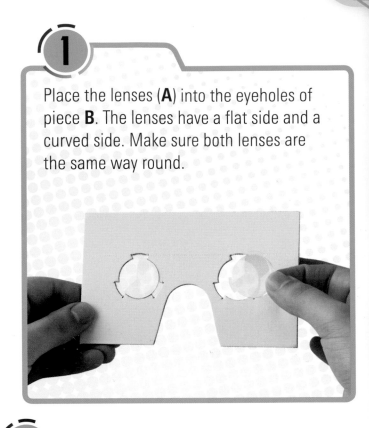

3

Place the piece with the lenses (**B**) into piece **C** so that the eyeholes line up. Pinch the bits of card with the empty eyeholes together so that **C** holds **B** in place.

The curved side of the lens should be on this side.

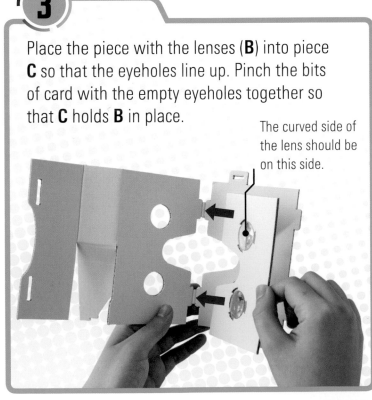

2

With the help of a ruler, carefully fold the fold lines of piece **C** as shown here. There are two places where you have to fold in the opposite direction to everywhere else. These folds have red dotted lines in this photo.

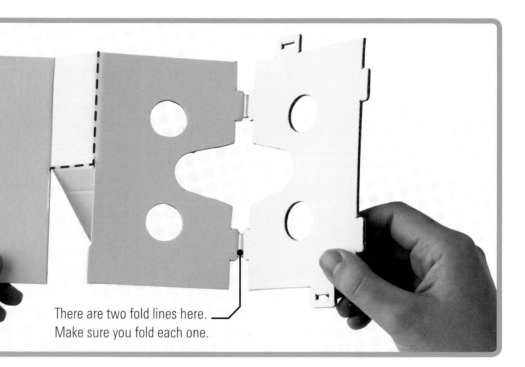

There are two fold lines here.
Make sure you fold each one.

4

Fold the fold lines of piece **D**. Fit the tabs below the eyeholes on **C** into the holes at the bottom of piece **D**. It should be tight – this is to hold everything in place.

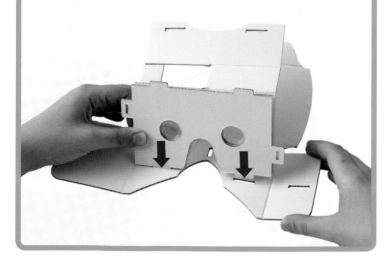

5

While carefully holding **C** in place, fit the downward facing tab in the middle of **C** into the small hole in **D**.

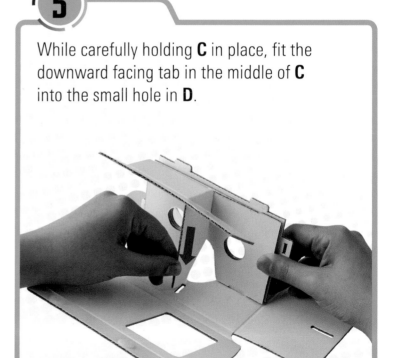

Instructions continue on the next page

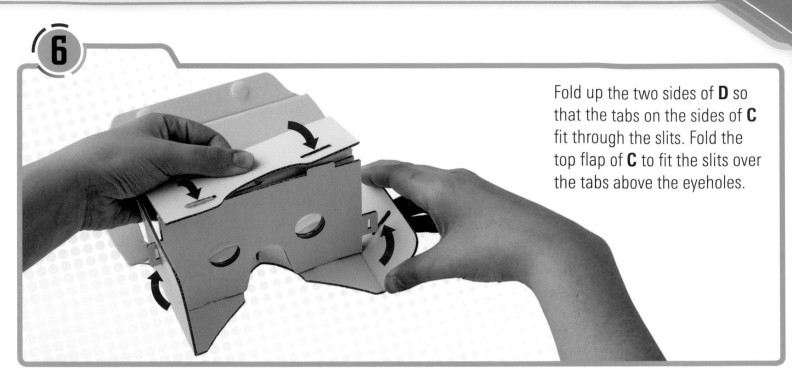

Fold up the two sides of **D** so that the tabs on the sides of **C** fit through the slits. Fold the top flap of **C** to fit the slits over the tabs above the eyeholes.

Fold the fold lines of piece **E**. Place **E** over the top of everything so that the tabs of **C** fit through the slits. Hold everything in place.

Put the lollipop-shaped tabs (**F**) into the tabs that stick out at the sides of the viewer. This will hold **E** in place. Then pull up the front flap of **D** and secure it to **E** using the little bits of Velcro®. Your viewer is now complete!

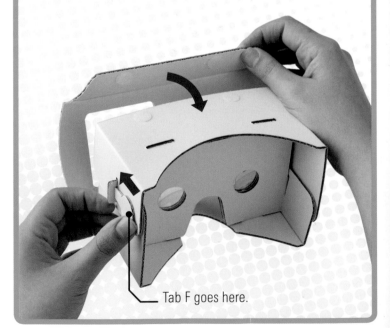

Tab F goes here.

How to use your viewer

⚠ Before using the viewer, please read the safety message on page 3.

1 Put phone in viewer

Open the app (see page 3 for download instructions) before carefully placing your smartphone in the viewer. The camera on the back of the phone needs to be able to see out of the hole at the front. The centre of the phone should line up with the central bit of cardboard.

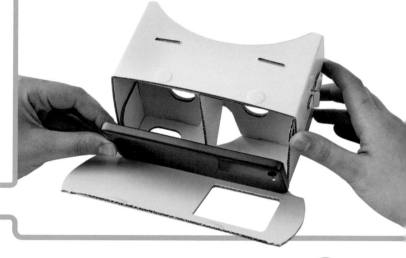

2 Look into viewer

Hold the viewer up to your face, making sure your hands are clasped around the outside so the phone is secure.

3 Scan trackers

When you spot a blue, circular tracker on a page, scan it with the camera to experience virtual reality! It may take your eyes a few seconds to adjust when first using the viewer.

This is one of the virtual reality trackers.

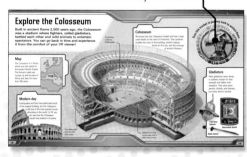

Face to face with T. rex

One of the largest and most powerful dinosaurs that ever lived, Tyrannosaurus rex would have made a terrifying sight. Now, thanks to virtual reality, you can travel 65 million years back in time and meet this fearsome dinosaur.

King of the dinosaurs

The word "rex" means king – and T. rex was the ruler of wherever it roamed. In the VR scene, you can see a T. rex threatening another dinosaur, Triceratops, which is guarding its nest of eggs.

With long, sharp teeth and powerful jaw muscles, T. rex's bite was its greatest weapon.

Spruce

Ginkgo

Fern

Creating the environment

The plants in the VR scene are the same as those that T. rex would have seen. We know this because scientists have found fossils of these plants from the right period. Some of these plants are still around today.

Scientists have found many complete fossilized T. rex skeletons.

T. rex tooth marks have been found on Triceratops bones.

The dinosaur is recreated on a computer as a 3D model.

Making the dino

The dinosaurs you can see in the VR app were created on a computer, as a 3D virtual model. The model is closely based on real dinosaur skeletons so all the measurements are accurate.

T. rex's heavy tail helped it balance, allowing it to walk on two legs.

Strong feet with spread-out toes supported the animal's enormous weight.

Scan this tracker to travel to the prehistoric world

How do we see in 3D?

A picture on a screen is two-dimensional, or 2D. The real world is 3D because it has an extra dimension: depth. Some things are far away, while others are much closer. For virtual reality to feel real, it has to be in 3D!

Each eye sees things differently. Your brain combines the two images to sense how far away the hand is.

How we see in 3D

We see in 3D because each of our eyes see what is around us slightly differently. See for yourself by doing this simple experiment.

Hold your hand in front of you and look at it with one eye open and then the other.

Right eye's view

Left eye's view

Recreating 3D

A virtual reality app shows what the left eye and the right eye would see if you were "inside" the virtual world. It displays each view on one side of the smartphone's screen, and when you use the viewer, each eye only sees one side.

Closer objects appear in a slightly different position in the left and right images.

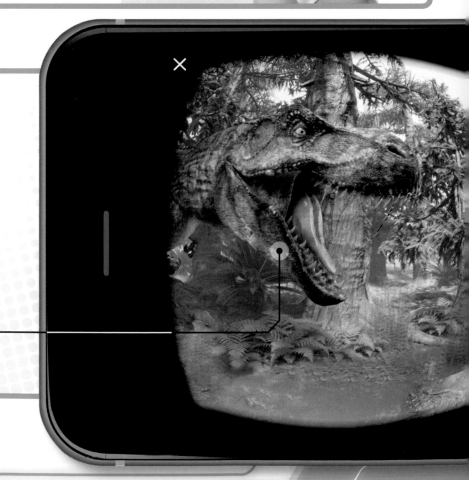

Using the viewer

When you look into the viewer, your eyes are close to the smartphone's screen. The lenses help your eyes to focus on the two images, so you really feel like you are inside a 3D world.

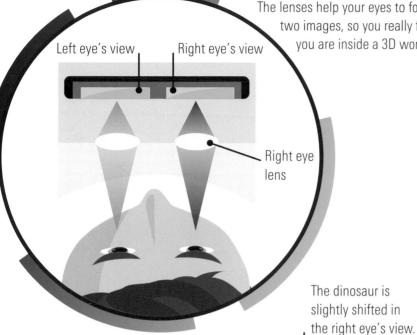

Left eye's view

Right eye's view

Right eye lens

The dinosaur is slightly shifted in the right eye's view.

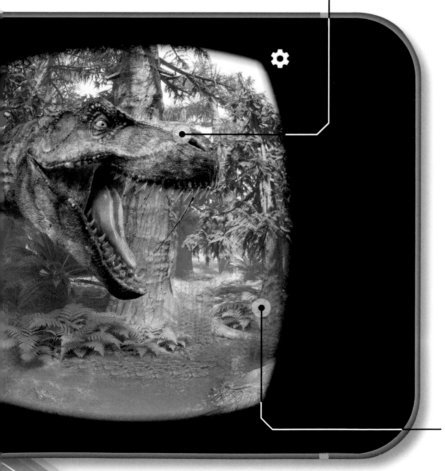

To see in 3D, each eye must see a slightly different view of the virtual world.

Looking around

A smartphone can tell what direction it is pointing. This makes it possible to look around in VR — another crucial part of creating the illusion of a 3D world.

More distant things, such as the trees, look the same in the two views.

Look inside a volcano

Volcanoes are both amazing and terrifying. When they erupt, hot liquified rock from deep underground, called magma, reaches the surface – sometimes violently. Get ready to explore one of the most dangerous places on Earth using VR.

There are more active volcanoes under the sea than on land.

Life of a volcano

Volcanoes are active, dormant, or extinct. Active volcanoes can erupt at any time, dormant volcanoes haven't been active for a while but could still erupt, and extinct volcanoes won't erupt again.

Magma chamber is full.

Active

Magma chamber is filling up.

Dormant

Magma chamber is empty.

Extinct

Dangerous eruption

When magma reaches the surface, it is called lava. Lava is so hot that it can destroy wildlife or villages. It explodes out and hardens, forming new layers, so the volcano grows bigger with each eruption.

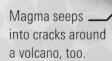

Magma seeps into cracks around a volcano, too.

Research drone

Scientists use drones to study volcanoes because it's often too dangerous for humans to get close. With VR, however, you can stand on the rim of an active volcano.

Chunks of flying lava are called lava bombs.

Some lava escapes through a secondary vent.

Scan this tracker to visit a volcano

How is a VR world created?

Some VR worlds are created from photographs, allowing you to visit real places without leaving home. But some, such as the ones in our app, are created using computer-generated imagery (CGI).

Planning a CGI world

1

Creating a convincing virtual world using CGI requires lots of research, talking, and thinking. Looking at real objects from different angles helps the team to visualize how a virtual world will work.

Making models

2

Virtual objects begin inside a computer as simple shapes, such as cubes, spheres, and cylinders. Designers change these into more complicated shapes — like dinosaurs!

Real objects, such as stuffed toys, help VR experts imagine how objects will look in a 3D environment.

Objects are first created as grey models.

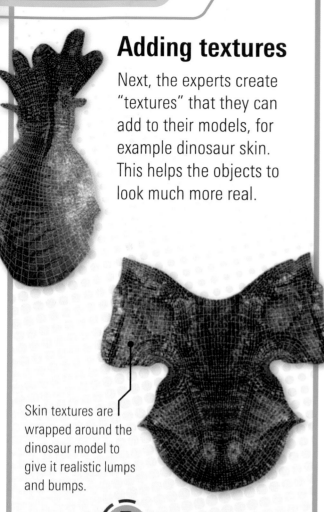

Adding textures

Next, the experts create "textures" that they can add to their models, for example dinosaur skin. This helps the objects to look much more real.

Skin textures are wrapped around the dinosaur model to give it realistic lumps and bumps.

3

Putting it all together

All the models the team have made – the dinosaurs, trees, plants, and rocks – are arranged in a scene. Then, the models are given their final appearance in a process called "rendering".

4

Surrounded

The scene is then placed on the inside surface of a sphere. In the VR world, the user looks out from the middle of this sphere, so they are completely surrounded by the environment.

5

The Triceratops is on one part of the sphere.

Explore the Colosseum

Built in ancient Rome 2,000 years ago, the Colosseum was a stadium where fighters, called gladiators, battled each other and wild animals to entertain spectators. You can go back in time and experience it from the comfort of your VR viewer!

The building could seat 50,000 people.

Map

The Colosseum is in Rome, which was the capital of the ancient Roman Empire. The Romans ruled over Europe, as well as parts of Africa and Asia, for more than 500 years.

Rome ●

Modern day

Earthquakes and fires have destroyed much of the original building, but the Colosseum is still one of the most popular tourist attractions in the world. In VR, you can see how the Colosseum would have looked in its prime.

The building had more than 200 stone arches.

Colosseum

We know how the Colosseum looked and how it was used thanks to the work of historians. They carefully studied the ruins of the building, ancient objects found on the site, and the writings of ancient Romans.

Scan this tracker to journey back to ancient Rome

Gladiators and wild animals were kept in cells under the floor.

Gladiators

Most gladiators were slaves or soldiers chosen for their strength and ability with weapons. They were given swords, shields, and helmets, but many died in combat.

Full-face helmet

Decorated shield

Steel sword

How does VR work on a smartphone?

A smartphone seems very clever when it runs a VR app – but a smartphone is a computer, and computers have to be told what to do. They follow long lists of instructions called computer programs, which are written by clever humans.

How it works

A smartphone carries out different parts of a program depending on information it receives. In a VR app, information comes from an accelerometer, a device that tells the phone which direction it's pointing.

Coding

A smartphone app is a computer program, written in computer code. Computer code is a list of instructions written in a special language that computers can follow.

The program asks simple questions which have "yes" or "no" answers to determine what to do next.

Is the smartphone pointing at the volcano for more than two seconds?

Yes

No

Reveal the inside of the volcano

Do nothing

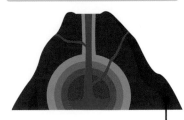

Point the smartphone at the volcano for more than two seconds to see inside the volcano.

If the smartphone isn't pointing at the volcano for two seconds nothing will happen.

Binary code

Inside a computer, programs are converted into a basic computer language – binary code. Binary code uses just two numbers: 0 and 1. These numbers are represented by electrical signals that can be "on" and "off".

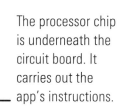

Electric current that is "on" represents binary "1".

Electric current that is "off" represents binary "0".

Inside your phone

The part of the phone that carries out instructions is called the processor chip. Inside the processor chip, billions of binary 1s and 0s whizz around as electric currents, representing the instructions and the information the program has received.

The processor chip is underneath the circuit board. It carries out the app's instructions.

Accelerometer chip sends information about the phone's position to the processor.

People who write computer programs are called "coders" or "programmers".

Visit a space station

Unless you train as an astronaut or you are incredibly rich, you will probably never travel to space. But with VR, you can blast off and explore the International Space Station (ISS) – the most expensive object ever built!

This robotic arm moves equipment and astronauts around outside the space station.

Above our heads

The ISS travels around Earth 400 km (250 miles) above the ground. The space station passes over a different part of Earth's surface on each pass.

The path of the ISS over Earth

Science in space

Astronauts live and work aboard the ISS for several months at a time. They carry out a range of scientific experiments – and enjoy a great view of planet Earth from space.

Building the ISS

The ISS was built in sections called modules. It took over 13 years to complete. The VR scene of the ISS took a few months to put together, following detailed plans.

Zarya module, 1998

Zvezda module, 2000

Laboratories, 2005

Completed, 2011

Huge solar panels provide power.

Dome-shaped observation module

Scan the tracker to fly into space

Dangerous journey

American and Russian rockets were used to lift each module of the ISS into space, and to take astronauts up there, too. You can get to the ISS just by looking into your VR viewer!

How can VR feel more real?

VR headsets are great for making you see things in a virtual world, but what about moving around or touching objects? Developers are working on clever bits of equipment that can make VR feel more real.

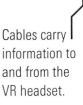

Cables carry information to and from the VR headset.

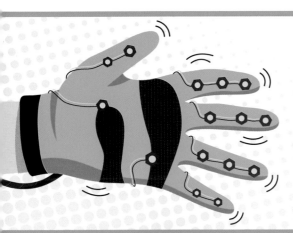

Haptic gloves

These specially designed gloves allow you to interact with virtual objects. "Haptic gloves" detect the positions of your fingers, and even put pressure on your fingertips to make you feel as though you are touching something.

Flying

When you shift your weight on this machine, sensors pass information to the computer. This movement is recreated in the virtual world so you feel like you are flying!

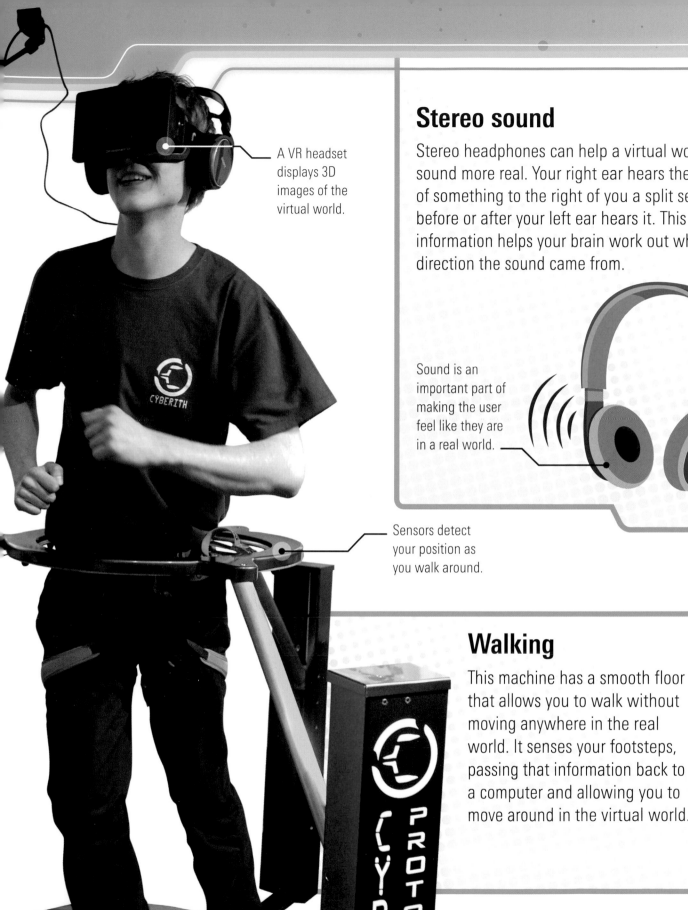

A VR headset displays 3D images of the virtual world.

Stereo sound

Stereo headphones can help a virtual world sound more real. Your right ear hears the sound of something to the right of you a split second before or after your left ear hears it. This information helps your brain work out which direction the sound came from.

Sound is an important part of making the user feel like they are in a real world.

Sensors detect your position as you walk around.

Walking

This machine has a smooth floor that allows you to walk without moving anywhere in the real world. It senses your footsteps, passing that information back to a computer and allowing you to move around in the virtual world.

A slippery surface allows the user to walk and detects their footsteps.

Jump into a pond

What better way to explore a pond than to shrink down to the size of an insect? With VR, you can do that! So get ready to experience a pond like never before.

A tadpole grows up to be a frog, with strong back legs that help it escape predators.

Grasses are very common on the banks of a pond.

A young dragonfly (a nymph) can eat tadpoles with its large jaws.

Pond life

A pond is home to many different kinds of life. There are amphibians, such as frogs, fish, and always lots of insects and plants.

Plants provide food and oxygen for underwater creatures.

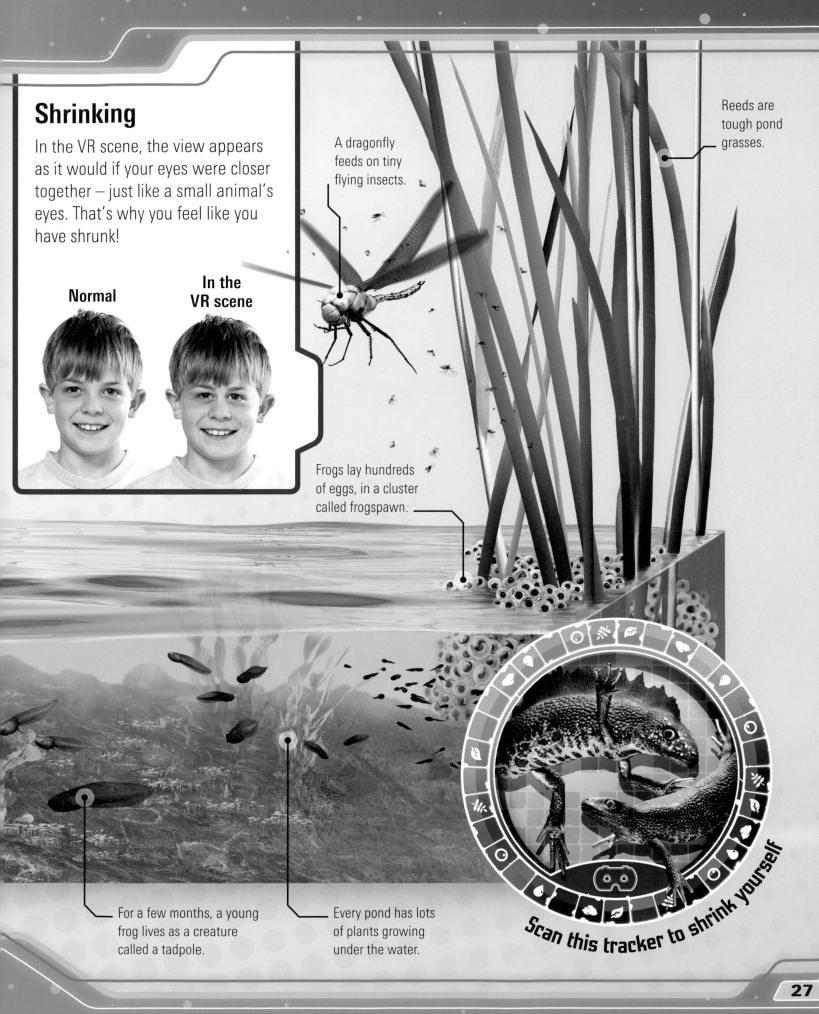

Shrinking

In the VR scene, the view appears as it would if your eyes were closer together – just like a small animal's eyes. That's why you feel like you have shrunk!

Normal

In the VR scene

A dragonfly feeds on tiny flying insects.

Reeds are tough pond grasses.

Frogs lay hundreds of eggs, in a cluster called frogspawn.

For a few months, a young frog lives as a creature called a tadpole.

Every pond has lots of plants growing under the water.

Scan this tracker to shrink yourself

Who uses VR?

Most people use VR for entertainment, such as computer games, or for education. But some people use it in their jobs. Here are just a few of the ways VR is used in the real world today, plus a glimpse into how it might be used in the future.

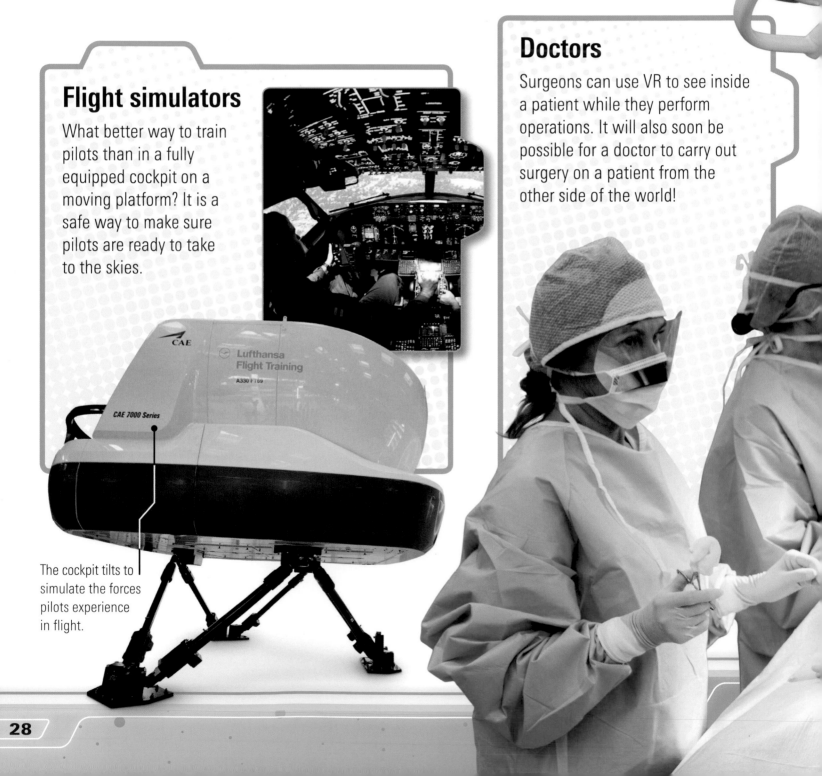

Flight simulators

What better way to train pilots than in a fully equipped cockpit on a moving platform? It is a safe way to make sure pilots are ready to take to the skies.

CAE
Lufthansa Flight Training
A330 FT69

CAE 7000 Series

The cockpit tilts to simulate the forces pilots experience in flight.

Doctors

Surgeons can use VR to see inside a patient while they perform operations. It will also soon be possible for a doctor to carry out surgery on a patient from the other side of the world!

Going out, staying in

In the future, it may be common to experience concerts or the theatre without leaving home. With a live feed of 3D images and sound, and a VR headset, you will feel like you are really there.

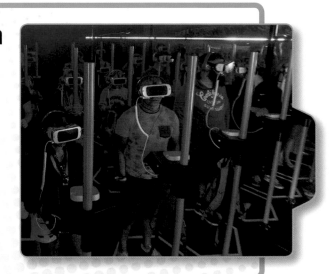

VR headset provides a live view inside the patient's body.

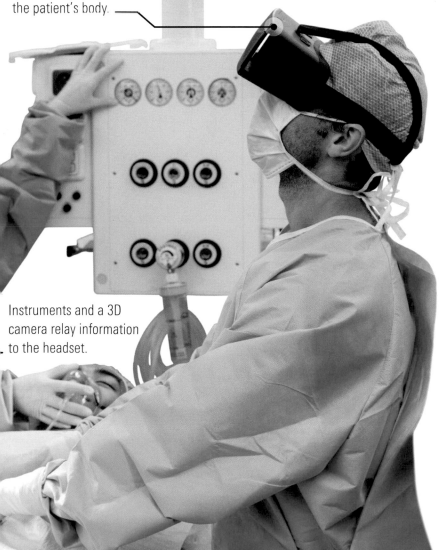

Instruments and a 3D camera relay information to the headset.

Augmented reality

"Augmented reality" is similar to VR. A smartphone, tablet, or VR headset displays computer-generated images over what you can see in the real world.

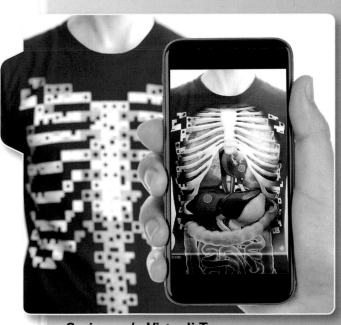

Curiscope's Virtuali-Tee

Glossary

2D
A "two-dimensional" image is a flat image, such as a photograph

3D
A "three-dimensional" image or object has depth – a sense of how close or far away things are

accelerometer
Part of a smartphone that senses which direction the phone is pointing

app
Computer program that can be downloaded and run on a smartphone

augmented reality (AR)
Technology similar to virtual reality in which virtual images appear over live images of the real world

binary code
System that only uses two digits, "0" and "1", to represent information. Computers work with binary code

CGI
Short for "computer-generated imagery". Any images created by a computer program

coder
Someone who writes computer programs. Also called a "programmer"

coding
Writing step-by-step instructions to tell a computer what to do

haptic gloves
Special gloves used in virtual reality to create a sensation of touch

lens
Clear glass or plastic object shaped in just the right way to focus on something. Lenses are found in glasses, telescopes, cameras, and virtual reality headsets

program
List of instructions carried out by a computer, written in computer code

reality
The real world that you live in

simulator
Any device that imitates part of the real world. A flight simulator is a virtual reality device that imitates flying a real aeroplane, and is used to train pilots

smartphone
Mobile phone that is also a computer. It can run many different kinds of app

virtual reality (VR)
A computer-generated world. You can experience virtual reality using a virtual reality headset

VR headset
Device, which covers your eyes, that you wear to experience virtual reality. Some headsets have screens built in, but with others you need to insert a smartphone to make them work

Index

Curiscope

Curiscope are on a mission to inspire curiosity. Founded in 2015 by Ben Kidd and Ed Barton, they are a world-leading virtual and augmented reality team based in Brighton, UK. Curiscope created one of the most watched virtual reality experiences of all time, an animated experience about great white sharks, as well as one of the most popular augmented reality products on the market, the Virtuali-Tee. Their passion for VR and AR stems from a belief that they are the perfect tools to unlock fascination for the wider world, helping people discover what they are truly interested in and inspiring them to do things they never believed they could do.

www.curiscope.com

Acknowledgements

DK would like to thank: Vijay Kandwal, Jaileen Kaur, and Neha Ahuja for design assistance, Jolyon Goddard for proofreading, Richard Leeney for photography, and Amias, Finn, Martha, Isabella, Jack, and Kathleen for modelling.

The publisher would like to thank the following for their kind permission to reproduce their photographs:

(Key: a-above; b-below/bottom; c-centre; f-far; l-left; r-right; t-top)

1 **123RF.com:** Adrian Buhai (cr, clb, c). 4 **123RF.com:** Adrian Buhai (cr); odmeyer (tl). 5 **123RF.com:** belikova (bl/Background); Adrian Buhai (cb). **Alamy Stock Photo:** ART Collection (cra); Reuters / Beck Diefenbach (br); Hugh Threlfall (fbr). **Curiscope:** (tc). **Fotolia:** Eric Isselee (bl/Cubs). **Getty Images:** Hulton Archive (cr); Allen J. Schaben / Los Angeles Times (crb). 9 **123RF.com:** Adrian Buhai (cb). 10-11 **Curiscope:** (c). 11 **123RF.com:** leonello calvetti (ca/T-Rex); Galina Peshkova (ca/Computer). **Curiscope:** (br). **Dorling Kindersley:** Senckenberg Gesellshaft Fuer Naturforschugn Museum (tr). 12 **Curiscope:** (br). 12-13 **Dreamstime.com:** Blackzheep (b/Phone). 13 **123RF.com:** Adrian Buhai (crb). **Curiscope:** (bl). 15 **Curiscope:** (cr). **Getty Images:** Ragnar Th. Sigurdsson (tr). 16 **Curiscope:** Autodesk screen shots reprinted courtesy of Autodesk, Inc. (cb). 17 **Curiscope:** (br); Autodesk screen shots reprinted courtesy of Autodesk, Inc. (cl, tr). 18-19 **TurboSquid:** Renderosi (c). 19 **Curiscope:** (tr). **TurboSquid:** Renderosi (tr/Gladiator). **Dorling Kindersley:** Ermine Street Guard (br). 20 **Alamy Stock Photo:** Andor Bujdoso (clb). 21 **123RF.com:** Sergey Sergeev (c). 22-23 **TurboSquid:** KuhnIndustries (c). 23 **NASA:** (tc, tc/Zvezda, tr/2005, tr/2011); Bill Ingalls (bc); **Curiscope** (crb). 24 **Getty Images:** DAVID MCNEW /

AFP (bl). 25 **Getty Images:** JEAN-FRANCOIS MONIER / AFP (l). 26-27 **TurboSquid:** (c). 27 **Curiscope:** (crb). 28 **Alamy Stock Photo:** PJF Military Collection (c); REUTERS (clb). 28-29 **Alamy Stock Photo:** Wavebreakmedia Ltd PH83 (c). 29 **Alamy Stock Photo:** WENN Ltd (cra). **Curiscope:** (crb/T-shirt). **Dreamstime.com:** Jannoon028 (crb/Mobile). 30 **123RF.com:** Adrian Buhai (br). 31 **123RF.com:** Adrian Buhai (bl, br). 32 **Curiscope:** (cra). 34 **Dorling Kindersley:** Andy Crawford (tl). **NASA:** (tc, c). 35 **Curiscope:** (All Images). 38 **123RF.com:** Andrey Egorov / Andrew7726 (bl/Used Twice, br/Used twice); Fred Weiss (cl/Used Twice). **Depositphotos Inc:** welcomia (br/Metal Background). **NASA:** (t, cr). 39 **123RF.com:** Andrey Egorov / Andrew7726 (t/Used Twice- Bullet Holes, b/Used Twice); Fred Weiss (cb). **Depositphotos Inc:** welcomia (t). **Dorling Kindersley:** Jon Hughes (cra). **Dreamstime.com:** Chachas (t/Used Thrice-Metal Wires, b). 42 **123RF.com:** Dirk Ercken / dirkercken (clb); Tom Grundy / pancaketom (cla); Christopher Ison / isonphoto (cb). **Dorling Kindersley:** Andy Crawford (br); Tim Ridley / Robert L. Braun (crb). **NASA:** (br/Astronaut); Jon Hughes (cr/Dinosaur). 43 **123RF.com:** Andrey Egorov / Andrew7726 (c/Used Thrice- Bullet Holes); Fred Weiss (t). **Depositphotos Inc:** welcomia (cl). **Dorling Kindersley:** Ermine Street Guard (tc, cra); Daniel Long (tr). **Dreamstime.com:** Chachas (c/Used Thrice). **NASA:** (bl)

Cover images: *Front:* **Curiscope:** cr; **Fotolia:** dundanim cl; **Getty Images:** a-r-t-i-s-t (Background); *Back:* **Curiscope:** bl; **Fotolia:** dundanim tc; **TurboSquid:** tl

All other images © Dorling Kindersley
For further information see: www.dkimages.com

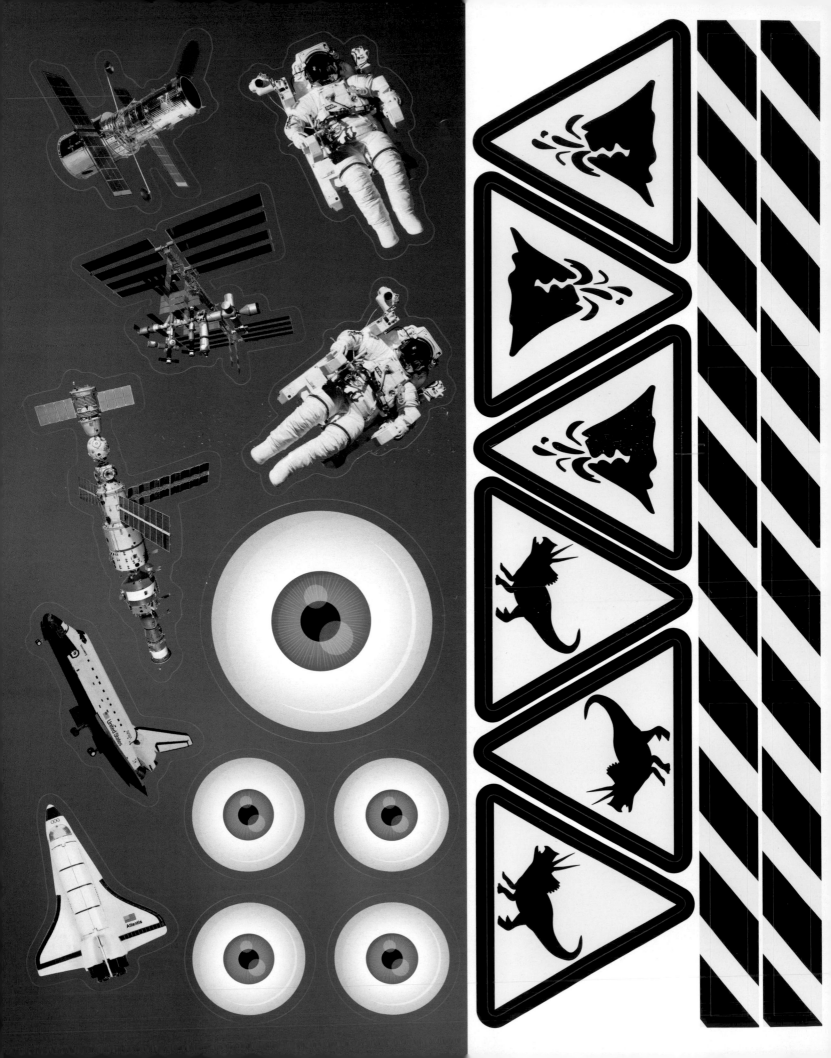

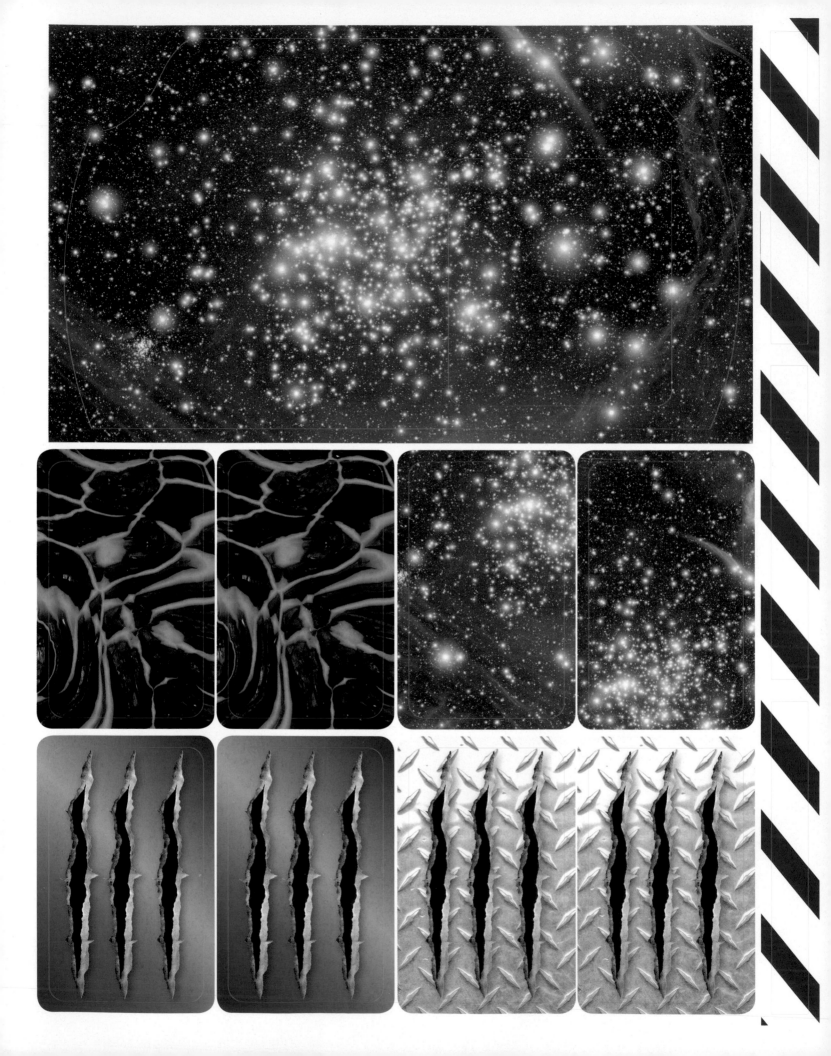

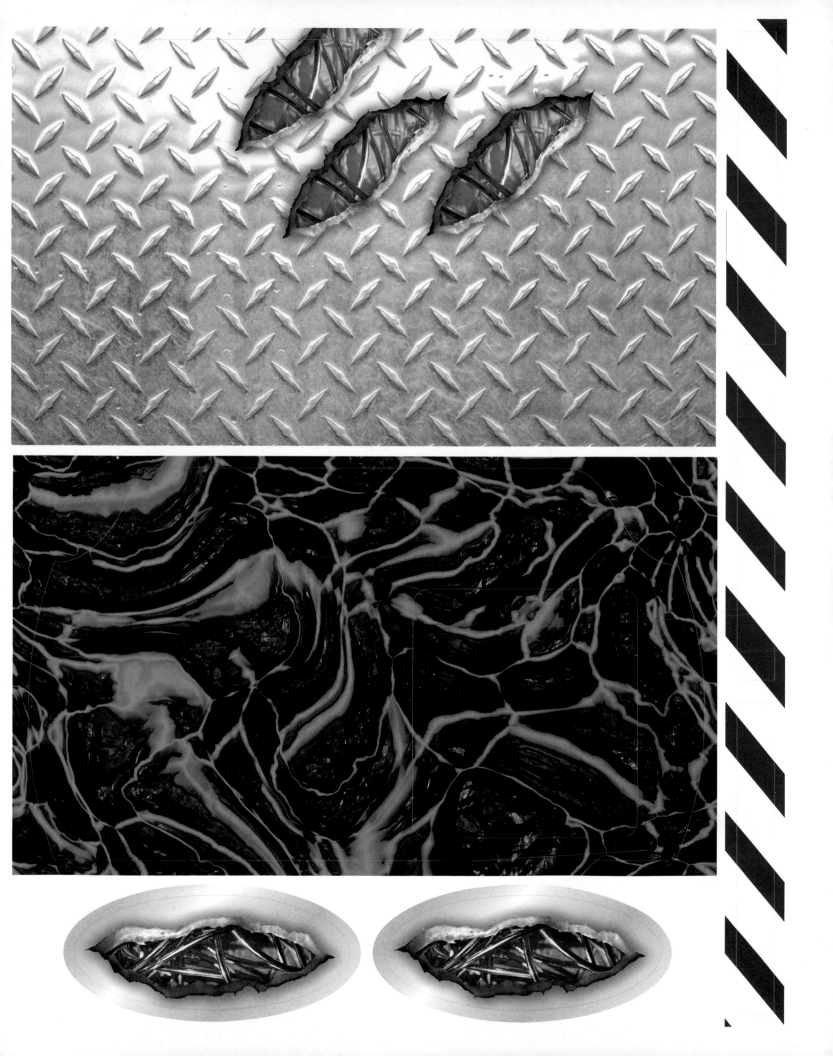